Ben Thornton

FRAGMENTS OF MY MIND

Limited Special Edition. No. 23 of 25 Paperbacks

Ben Thornton was born in 2000 in Tunbridge Wells, Kent. He attended The Skinners' School from age 11–18 where his passion for english and poetry ignited. Opting to pursue this interest further, Ben wrote this debut collection whilst studying english literature at the University of East Anglia at the age of 18.

For Mum, Dad and Grace

Ben Thornton

FRAGMENTS OF MY MIND

AUSTIN MACAULEY PUBLISHERS™

LONDON • CAMBRIDGE • NEW YORK • SHARJAH

A CIP catalogue record for this title is available from the British Library.

ISBN 9781528986144 (Paperback)
ISBN 9781528986151 (ePub e-book)

www.austinmacauley.com

First Published (2020)
Austin Macauley Publishers Ltd
25 Canada Square
Canary Wharf
London
E14 5LQ

The Unknown

I heard a whisper in my ear
But no one seemed to be near.

I edged towards a warm, white glow
And found myself lost amongst the unknown.

A sudden nerve took over my body.

A warm gust occupied the air
As I wondered why I was there.

A big booming voice from above
Possessing a tone none other than love.
"Don't be afraid," the booming voice cried
"You're in a better place now."
I knew I had died…

A sudden rush
Flowed through my veins
As I came back to Earth
To witness what remains.

I searched and searched
But all I could see
A plaque that lay there
Dedicated to me.

Up There

In the attic where no one is seen
The voices in my head become a distant dream.

The thud of the stairs below
As I look out the window.

The sound of the floorboards creaking
Disrupts my intense thinking.

As I wonder…

The clock keeps ticking
In a box in the corner
Unaware of the horror
About to occur.

The steps become louder
As no one allowed her
To come near.

The rattle of the door frame
As I wonder
Am I sane?

I wake up in a hospital bed
And wonder
Was that all in my head?

The House at the End of the Road

No! No!
Don't Go Near.
Little boy George disappeared here.

All concerns put aside
The boys braved it
And dared to go inside.

The floorboards began creaking
As the boys started freaking.

Blood in the kitchen sink tipped the boys
Onto the brink
Of madness.

An evil possessed them
As they turned towards the door
A figure stood before them
None other
Than little boy George.

"Welcome," the little boy hissed.

As the boys ran to hide
It occurred to them
They should not have gone inside.

The Desert Land

I surge across the African valley
The echoes of a tribal rally
Ring across the desert land.

I ponder
And decide to wander
Over to the banging of the drums.

I cross the vast emptiness
Over the desert plains.
I'm not sure how long I walked for
But seemed like days and days.

I walked and walked
Slower and slower.

The sand around me started to spin
The fatigue was beginning to settle in.

My eyes began to close.
How I longed to be home.

The soft whisper of voices in my ear
A group of people seemed to be near.

Their voices were muffled
But some words were clear.
"Come and help him!
He's here! He's here!"

Ray of Light

A complex emotion
That no one really understands.

The warm feeling from inside
What's mine is yours
And what's yours is mine.

The light at the end of a dark tunnel
A friendly face at a time of need.

Memories made and laughter shared
Eternally grateful for the experiences
And care.

A rescuer from dismay
A creator of the man I am today.

Escape

Years ago
I gave into the pressure
Amounting on me.
I took them
And this is my story.

They numbed the pain
The heartbreak
The constant questioning
Am I good enough?
Is life worth it?

They took me out of misery whilst
Admittedly
Threw me deeper towards the steep slope
Of addiction.

Ten years clean
And I look back on my experience.

A distraction is not the answer.

My past may be blurred
But I'm doing my best
To make my experiences heard.

A Childhood Summer

Early mornings.
Late evenings.
Apples growing on the tree outside
Birds chirping from the early hours.

The sound of ice cream vans
Calliopes, twisters, 90s.

The eagerly awaited holiday
To the coast
Cornwall, Devon.

A swim in the sea
A chip shop for tea!

The childhood memories
The excited feeling
Has never sounded
More appealing.

A Final Visit

I awoke with the sound
Of the dog barking downstairs.

I venture down.
The barking stops.
There's no problem down here.

The sound of a glass smashing
Against the tiled kitchen floor
Wakes me up again.

I edge down the stairs
More cautious this time
But again
There's no problem down here.

At the top of the stairs
I see writing
On my bedroom door
And hear running
Across the hallway floor.

I fall back asleep and awake the next morning
I look to my left
My wife's laying there snoring.

I get ready for the day
Forgetting what happened last night.
She bolted up in bed
"Is my aunt alright?"

We drive to the home
And search for Aunt May.
We receive the dreaded news
"She's passed away."

The moment sank in
And it became clear.
The writing on the door...
'Goodbye Dear'.

Friday the 13th

I remember it like it was yesterday
The events of Friday the 13th
Three years ago.

An Ouija board sat in front of me
The temptation was overwhelming and
Eventually I gave in.

The regret was instant.
The lights began to flicker.
I felt a warm breath
Down the back of my neck.
My name rung around the room.
I asked who was present in the room
When

The board began to spell out a name.
The familiar name of my uncle.
Fear struck my body.

"Come downstairs," my mother cried.

The lights went out.

My uncle had suddenly died.

Mental Prison

The constant questioning
Of the world around you.
Unable to keep track
Of who
You really are.

Trapped within your mind
Unable to leave things behind
In the past.

The difficulty of reaching out
And admitting
You need help.

Reach out and ask
For guidance.

A problem shared
Is a problem halved

And

Most importantly

You are not alone.

The Woods

Ever since I was a young boy
My parents warned me
Never to venture
Into those woods.

I was fifteen years old
An only child
When I finally dared
To go beyond the line of the trees
Against my parents' word
And into the woods.

The events of that day
Were indescribable.

The woods had four graves
And had eerie, external presence
Amongst the trees.

The sounds of leaves shuffling
And muffled voices
A few steps away.

I edged towards the voices
And everything became clear.
Stood there were my parents and a shovel.
"Your siblings are buried here."

UFO

It was a cloudy night
As I wandered towards a glow
In the distance.

The gentle whir of the air around me
Became louder
And louder
And louder.

The glow became brighter
As I began to feel
Possessed by an external force.

I woke up restrained
With unusual faces around me
Uttering words in a foreign language
Discussing issues amongst themselves.

The sound of leaking gas
Forced my eyes shut.

My memory may be blurred
But I know what I saw
On the night of the 23rd.

Unique

I write and write
But nothing flows
When the question was there
My hands froze.

x-y
2+3
Maths
Is not for me.

Don't panic
Don't be scared
Students across the world
Are always compared.

Competition is intense
Stay true to your skills
And some time or another
You'll afford those huge bills.

The Neighbourhood

I hear a scream from the floor below
Gunshots out the window.

Alarms start ringing
Families clinging…
Together.

Madness ensues
But everyone knows
This town has issues.

Cars race around the block
Chased by police
All the way to the dock.

Cargo is loaded
Onto the back of ships.
Only a few know what lies inside
Those containers.

I check the kids are still sleeping…
I find them weeping.

"Am I safe here?"
"What's happening outside?"
Are the questions I'm asked.

Unsure what to reply
I kiss them goodnight
And tell them not to cry.

Dark Side of Love

Knock, knock, knock
At the door.
"We're looking for Bill."
"He doesn't live here anymore."

Bill was my husband
But left years ago.
We argued and argued
But where did he go?

He came home late
Every evening
But when I questioned
He threatened leaving.

I needed the money
I couldn't let him leave.
All throughout our marriage
He forced me to grieve.

His job was unknown
He handed me coins.
In exchange
He exploited my loins.

He left one day
And never came back.
I'm no longer worried
Over the threat of his attack.

The police sat me down
And quizzed his hiding
But were unsatisfied
With the answers I was providing.

I wish I knew
Where my husband was.
And by the looks of things
So did the law.

The door swung open
And I heard Bill's cry:
"Don't answer anything.
I swear I'm a good guy."

1st of April

I go to scream
But nothing comes out.

My hands are tied
My legs stuck
To the ground.

The room is dark and empty
And dead
Silent.

Footsteps begin outside
Muffled voices become clear:
"Sssh…Sssh!
He's in here!"

The doors fly open
Sunlight becomes seen
I recognise the voices
But what does this all mean?

I'm hit with confusion
Fear and anxiety.

I open my eyes.
I am in a great hall.
The voices roar with laughter
"Happy April Fools!"

Blaze

I walk across the panicked street
Sirens ringing, people running.
Sweat dripping from the heat
Of the fire.

"An attack," they said
Several people scampering
Away from the building
Away from the blaze.

Debris falling.
People weeping.
Ambulances, fire engines, police cars
Flood the scene.

What lies before me
I can never unsee.

We all back
The victims
Of this attack.

Murder

The phone started ringing
Seven in the morning
Who could it be?
The police were on the phone…
They were looking for me.

I drove to the station
To which I was greeted
"Please be patient."
Everything seemed heated…

They drove to me to the park
The cloudless sky lighting up the trees
Surrounding me.
Tape was everywhere
Reporters stood ready
For their prey.

The police finally broke the tense silence
"A body was found in the early hours.
It was the body of your brother."

I became numb
And to make matters worse
The policeman revealed
I was prime suspect for his murder.

Weeks went by
Awaiting the trial.
I was full of fear, anxiety
And denial.

I stood there in court
The judge began speaking.
I was guilty of murder.
I started freaking.

I was sentenced to life.

I rolled up at the prison
Got into my cell.
Thoughts bouncing around my head
I was living in hell.

Ten years went by
I couldn't handle my life.
My last resort
To get hold of a knife.

I cut and cut
And enjoyed the bleeding.
My mind was delicate
And I refused feeding.

The inevitable occurred
And I died on
June the 23rd.

I rose to heaven
And in the distance stood
My brother.

The first thing I asked
"Why am I in heaven?"
My brother looked stern
"It wasn't your fault."

The Previous Resident

Shadows move over
The bedroom wall
Spelling out names
I'd never seen before.

I lie there
Looking at the ceiling
Reading the names
Confused.

A message appears:
"Go outside."
To which I adhere…
I stood in the cold, brisk night.

A shovel lays at my feet
Encouraging me to dig beneath.

I reach a wooden box
Wary of what's inside.
I open the lid
A body is before me.

A note folded amongst the heap
"Congratulations" it read
"they encouraged you to dig."

I wondered who wrote
This eerie note.

A message came back
A few days later.
"You're next"
Read the message from the hater.

The previous resident
Was known for his actions.
I was obviously
His next interaction.

Revenge

The clock struck twelve
And I bolted upright in bed.
It was time.

I put on my uniform.
All black.
I can't be seen.

I drove to the point
Looking over Hyde park.
He was due to walk past
Any minute.

There he was.
I saw him in the distance.
I loaded my gun.
Took aim.
BANG.

I missed.

Disappointed in myself
I fled the scene.
I will try again tomorrow.
He knows what he's done.
He will pay for what he's done.
I will get revenge.

I resumed my sleep.